Explaining
Church
Discipline

Stuart Murray

Sovereign World

Bible quotations are taken from
the NIV The Holy Bible, New International Version.
© Copyright 1973, 1978, 1984 International Bible Society.
Published by Hodder & Stoughton.

ISBN: 1 85240 134 6

SOVEREIGN WORLD LIMITED
P.O. Box 777, Tonbridge, Kent TN11 9XT, England.

Typeset and printed in the UK by Sussex Litho Ltd, Chichester, West Sussex.

Contents

Contents

Preface

"What are you writing about?" asked Jeannie, when she discovered I was writing another book.

"Church discipline", I replied.

"Oh horrors!" was her immediate response.

The subject of church discipline seems to provoke such reactions. Bad experiences or unpleasant stories of church discipline being exercised in heavy-handed or unwise ways have caused many Christians to give it a wide berth. But the absence of church discipline is much more damaging to Christians and churches. Church discipline is an expression of Christian love and an important aspect of making disciples. The words "discipline" and "discipleship" are connected: exercising discipline in the church is part of discipling one another. Those in the business of making disciples deprive themselves and their churches of tremendous opportunities for spiritual growth if they ignore church discipline. My hope for this book is that the way biblical church discipline is explained here will allay fears and help churches to restore this vital practice.

Thanks are due to a number of friends who read through earlier drafts of what you have here and made various helpful comments: Terry Brewer, Nigel Wright, Mike Wood and especially my wife, Rachel. Thanks also to Jeannie for alerting me to the strength of reaction to this subject. To her and many whose reaction is similar I offer this study.

1

The History of
Church Discipline

*Go and make disciples of all nations, baptising them in the
name of the Father and of the Son and of the Holy Spirit,
and teaching them to obey everything I have commanded
you.* (Matthew 28:19-20)

These words were ringing in the ears of the eleven disciples as
they watched their Lord leave them. *"Go and make disciples."*
Not just believers or converts, not church attenders or even
church members, but disciples. A daunting task for this uncertain
and fearful group, especially since Jesus clearly expected them to
do this on a worldwide scale.

They knew what disciples were, of course, for they were
disciples themselves. Disciples were learners, apprentices,
followers, those who had committed their lives to seeking first
God's kingdom. And they knew what discipleship involved:
listening to Jesus, obeying him, making hard choices, setting
aside other loyalties, learning from mistakes, facing hardships.
They had chosen to be disciples. Now they were to call others to
this costly way of discipleship.

How? By proclaiming Christ, baptising those who responded
and teaching them what it meant to follow Jesus. In their
preaching and conversations they would explain that Jesus
wanted disciples who would be serious about following him.
Baptism would be the sign of becoming a disciple and of joining
a community of other disciples. Jesus' teachings would guide
these new communities, and their members would be responsible
for helping each other become – and remain – disciples.

That was the strategy and when the Holy Spirit came a few
days later they had about 3000 men and women in their

discipleship classes. In the early chapters of Acts, Luke provides fascinating glimpses of this young church in action (Acts 2-4). Numbers were increasing rapidly but the task of "making disciples" was not forgotten. They met in each others' homes, broke bread together, learned and worshipped together, prayed for one another and welcomed others who wanted to become disciples. They explored economic aspects of discipleship as they sold their possessions and shared with those in need. They saw great miracles taking place. And they grew bolder in their witness as the Spirit filled them.

Luke also records struggles and setbacks: the dishonesty of Ananias and Sapphira (Acts 5), ethnic squabbling over food allocation (Acts 6), persecution and martyrdom (Acts 7, 8), the apostles' slowness to reach out to the Gentiles (Acts 11). Any of these factors could have jeopardised the young movement. But the way in which they faced these challenges ensured instead that they resulted in growth and renewed discipleship. Dishonesty was confronted, disunity was repaired, and opposition was turned into opportunity. This was no perfect church but it was a community that took discipleship seriously – and recognised that discipleship could not be separated from discipline.

From Jerusalem the movement spread all over the known world. Thousands of new churches were established. The rest of the New Testament introduces us to just a handful of these churches and their struggle to be faithful communities of disciples. They continued to baptise those who joined them and to teach them what Jesus had commanded. Discipleship was expected and the churches were generally held in high regard, even by their opponents, because of their quality of life and relationships.

But these were not perfect churches, and we read of church members teaching false doctrines, falling out with each other and living in ways that were clearly contrary to Jesus' teachings. How these churches tackled such problems were as crucial for their health and continued growth as was the way the Jerusalem church had faced setbacks and challenges. Church discipline was crucial. When things went wrong, when relationships became strained, when behaviour fell short of Christian standards, when the church's witness was compromised, the community had a responsibility to act.

There was sometimes an understandable reticence to act. After all, they had experienced the unconditional love of God. Jesus had warned against judging one another and had spoken about forgiving over and over again. Their mission was to reach out in accepting and welcoming love to their neighbours. How did church discipline fit in? But their mandate was to make disciples and making disciples sometimes involved discipline. Without this they would have lost the distinctive testimony that was attractive and challenging to their contemporaries. They would also have failed their own fellow-disciples just when they most needed the help of the community.

Furthermore, exercising discipline within the Christian community was something Jesus himself had taught and modelled. On several occasions he confronted, admonished and corrected his disciples. He rebuked Peter for becoming a stumbling-block (Matthew 16:23); those who stopped children from coming to him were gently reprimanded (Matthew 19:14); disunity among the disciples was quashed by a challenge to servant leadership (Matthew 20:24-28). And on one of the few occasions we hear him talking about the church, he described a community that cared enough to confront one another and exercise discipline (Matthew 18:15-17). For those who took Jesus seriously, there was no avoiding the connection between discipleship and church discipline. And the rest of the New Testament confirms that the disciples realised this and taught the churches they planted to exercise church discipline.

Making disciples involves more than discipline. Proclaiming a full gospel that asserts the Lordship of Christ, restoring baptism in water and in the Spirit as vital components in the process of becoming disciples, taking seriously the teaching of Jesus and rediscovering the church as a community of disciples are all involved. But discipline is also crucial.

Nor is church discipline the only form of discipline. The New Testament speaks also about self-discipline; about spiritual disciplines such as prayer and fasting, Bible study and gathering for worship; and about God disciplining his children. But church discipline is an important aspect of discipline (sometimes distinguished from other aspects as "corrective" or "remedial" discipline) – and one that has often been neglected or misunderstood.

To understand why church discipline has been neglected, we will delve briefly into the history of the church. Whether we realise it or not, our practices are influenced by events that happened long ago and far away.

As we have seen, Jesus' disciples taught the churches they planted how church discipline was to be practised. They laid good foundations and for the following 250 years most churches continued to exercise church discipline. There was tremendous concern for holiness, and discipleship was taken seriously. But church discipline was not always exercised wisely. Somehow forgiveness and the restoration of those who had been disciplined began to be neglected. Controversies raged about whether those who had wavered under persecution could be readmitted to church membership, and about whether sins committed after baptism could be forgiven. The power of church discipline to heal and restore was being lost. Church discipline was becoming a threat rather than an expression of fellowship.

Early in the fourth century, radical changes took place. Christianity was adopted as the state religion by the Roman emperor, Constantine, and the development of "Christian Europe" or Christendom began. Church and society were no longer distinct and the power of the state was used to enforce conformity. This made the practice of biblical church discipline almost impossible. In the fourth century, the churches experienced enormous changes as they adjusted from being a powerless and persecuted minority but with a distinctive lifestyle, to a privileged and persecuting majority that was almost indistinct from the rest of society. Church discipline was one of many casualties.

Making disciples was largely abandoned in favour of creating a society where nominal Christianity provided the religious glue that held the empire together. Church discipline was concerned now with dealing with threats to this arrangement, and the methods used were punitive and violent. If there is no distinction between church and society, putting someone out of the church involves putting them out of society as well – by imprisonment or execution. Church discipline became an oppressive practice used against non-conformists that in time produced the horrors of the Inquisition.

But sporadically, during the next 1000 years, groups of Christians emerged who were unhappy with this nominal Christianity and longed to restore New Testament Christianity – including proper church discipline. These groups were regarded as threats to the status quo, as heretics and traitors. They were dismissed as arrogant perfectionists and violently suppressed. But they represented an alternative tradition that refused to let slip a vision of the church as a voluntary community of disciples. They practised church discipline. Sometimes they did this unwisely and became legalistic and harsh as some of the early churches had. They were criticised for this – by those whose version of church discipline was to torture and execute them! But they maintained a persistent witness to the Christian life as discipleship and to the role of church discipline in helping each other follow Jesus.

In the early stages of many renewal movements church discipline was rediscovered. The medieval Waldensians in their Alpine valleys restored church discipline. The sixteenth century Anabaptists recovered it in central Europe. The Moravians and their most famous convert, John Wesley, practised it in the seventeenth century. Church discipline was a familiar feature of English Baptist churches in the eighteenth century and of Brethren churches in the nineteenth century. Both the Welsh revival and the East African revival in the twentieth century practised it.

Indeed, whenever discipleship is taken seriously, this neglected subject is rediscovered. Where Christianity is nominal, where church and society are indistinct, where state power is used to enforce religious conformity, where the Christendom model is operating, church discipline will generally be absent or punitive. John Calvin's attempt to impose church discipline in Geneva during the Reformation shows how difficult this is under a state church system. But wherever Christians recall Jesus' command to go and make disciples and set about building communities where membership is voluntary and where discipleship is taken seriously, the kind of church discipline that Jesus taught reappears.

The purpose of this book is to explain what the New Testament teaches about church discipline. I have been involved in planting and leading a church where church discipline was operating and I have seen its benefits. What I am describing here, however, goes beyond my experience in that church. In part it comes out of reflecting on how we might have practised church discipline more effectively; in part on the experience of others, in conversation and testimonies. I write as one involved in training church planters and church leaders. I am concerned that most church leaders receive no instruction in this area. Consequently, in many churches there is no framework for church discipline. When problems arise, biblical principles are ignored or misapplied. But properly understood and wisely practised, church discipline is good news, a crucial aspect of the church's response to its commission to "go and make disciples".

2

The Neglect of Church Discipline

Why is the subject of church discipline rarely included in church teaching programmes? Why isn't it on the agenda of leadership training courses? The absence of such teaching means that churches and their leaders are ill-equipped to handle situations that require church discipline. Lacking a biblical framework and not having thought through what is involved, leaders may react either by failing to exercise discipline or by exercising it in a heavy-handed and unhelpful way. Church members with little understanding of church discipline may take sides so that any attempt to exercise church discipline is ineffective.

When church discipline in such situations proves to be anything but a positive experience, the church and its leaders become wary of going through the process again. A vicious circle forms where church discipline is never practised properly. Ignoring the subject seems better than trying and failing to make it work. And so church discipline is not taught and when the next crisis arrives, there is still no framework for dealing with it. Any mention of the subject produces a negative reaction.

Misunderstandings and bad experiences of church discipline offer one explanation of why a subject so widely discussed in the New Testament is so neglected by the churches. Even where people have not had a personal experience of church discipline going wrong, they have heard of situations where it did. Heavy-handed leadership, divided congregations, harsh words and unresolved issues are reported. Examining church history, as we have seen, uncovers a similar story. Many groups that did attempt to practise church discipline appear rather narrow, perfectionist and intolerant. Church discipline has received a bad name because of the ways in which it has been exercised.

But the testimony of the whole New Testament is that church discipline is important and beneficial for church life. There is an embarrassing amount of teaching on this topic, which is hard to ignore. The Gospels of Matthew and Luke both record Jesus' teaching about church discipline. Paul deals with the issue in almost all of his letters to churches – to the Romans, the Corinthians, the Galatians, the Philippians, the Colossians and the Thessalonians – and in his correspondence with Timothy and Titus. Indeed, his letters to Corinth can be regarded as church discipline in written form as he confronts and admonishes the church on a wide range of issues. Peter, John and Jude all warn their readers to be on guard against those who would damage the church. And the letters to the churches in Revelation contain several references to the practice of church discipline or the need for it. In almost every strand of New Testament teaching church discipline is taught.

Why, then, do so many churches continue to ignore this? Inadequate teaching and bad experiences have already been suggested as factors, but there are others:

(1) Cultural factors. Contemporary Western culture prides itself on being liberal and tolerant of everything except intolerance. The individual is responsible for deciding how to live and nobody has the right to challenge this. The idea of absolute standards and of being part of a community where there is accountability to one another does not fit well into this non-confrontational cultural climate. Churches that practise church discipline may be regarded as sects. Practising church discipline may require churches to embrace the reality of being counter-cultural.

(2) Fear. Exercising church discipline is not easy. Confronting people and admonishing them, talking about sin and compromise is quite daunting. We risk becoming unpopular, alienating people, suffering insults and retaliation. In some countries we may face litigation. There is also the possibility of making mistakes, of misreading situations, of handling the process badly. This fear can prevent us from acting.

(3) Concern about being judgemental. This may simply be a

14

reflection of our tolerance culture or of the fears we have identified. Or it may be a valid concern that many churches seem judgemental and quick to condemn people. Exercising church discipline might make things worse. This is an important issue, which we will explore below. Many churches desperately need to become communities where unconditional love, acceptance and forgiveness are practised. But to see church discipline as a step in the opposite direction is seriously to misunderstand the purpose and nature of church discipline. As we shall see, exercising church discipline properly is a step away from being judgemental, a powerful expression of Christian love.

(4) Unrealistic expectations of preaching and spiritual experiences. In some churches preaching and teaching is central and the expectation seems to be that this alone will produce disciples. In other churches a similar expectation is placed on charismatic gifts or spiritual experiences. There may be little patience with suggestions that counselling may be helpful or that a process of discipline might be used. I do not wish to disparage the influence of teaching or spiritual experiences, both of which are vital in making disciples. But I am not persuaded that the expectations are realistic or that the results justify setting aside the often more costly and time-consuming aspects of making disciples.

(5) Declining numbers. In many Western nations, churches are losing members rather than gaining them. This is true not only in Europe but even in North America, despite all the teaching on church growth and the fame of certain mega-churches. Much of the growth that is taking place is no more than members transferring from one church to another. This affects the exercise of church discipline in two ways. First, when your numbers are declining, the prospect of reducing them further by putting people out of the church is not particularly welcome. Second, in an era of consumer choice churchgoing, church discipline is not easy to exercise if the church member involved can simply join the church down the road.

There is no easy answer to the second problem. Only if there is trust and fellowship between churches and their leaders can church discipline be exercised effectively. However, the possibility that someone disciplined by a church might join the church down the road does not absolve the church of its responsibility to exercise discipline. How the person who is being disciplined responds and how other churches react is a separate issue, albeit an important one.

With regard to the first issue, it may be hard for a declining church to accept, but exercising discipline may have a positive effect on church growth. Evidence from many cultures suggests this is the case. A church that is prepared to show that it takes discipleship seriously may be surprisingly attractive. Churches that care enough for their members to confront them when necessary and exercise church discipline rather than allowing relationships to be soured and issues unresolved have a distinctive testimony that may be counter-cultural but is much closer to the radical Christianity of the New Testament. This Christianity may be offensive to religious consumers but it has always attracted those who are serious about following Jesus.

Despite the difficulties and discouragements we have recognised, it is important that the practice of church discipline is recovered. Although this is not on the agenda of many churches, there are signs of hope and windows of opportunity:

(a) The fact that church discipline is taught throughout the New Testament means that those who read their Bibles keep coming up against it. Many Christians suspect that this subject is important even if they are unsure what to do about it. I have discovered that talking about it, especially with church leaders, often produces reactions along the lines of "Yes, we haven't really looked at this properly. Perhaps we ought to do something about it."

(b) Until relatively recently the state-church model has predominated in many nations. As we have seen, where there is no clear distinction between church and society, biblical church discipline is difficult to exercise. Several Protestant Reformers toyed with church discipline but concluded it was impractical. Trapped in the state-church system they were unable to implement what they read in the Bible. It was left to the Anabaptists, who rejected this system in favour of voluntary churches made up of would-be disciples, to show that it was both practical and vital. But the demise of Christendom in many nations, and the recovery of the kind of church described in the New Testament – a believers' church or community of disciples – as the normal form of church life, makes the recovery of New Testament church discipline feasible. Today even churches that are still officially "established" are increasingly adopting practices that were once restricted to groups they dismissed as sects.

(c) In the United Kingdom and elsewhere in the world the so-called "House Church Movement" has significantly impacted the thinking and practice of the church at large. A distinctive feature of these churches is their emphasis on discipleship and practice of church discipline. Although they have frequently been criticised, sometimes unfairly, for the way in which they have exercised church discipline, their example has put the subject back on the agenda for other churches, even if concerns about how this is practised have caused many to hesitate before going further. However, once the subject is on the agenda, other churches may discover that it is not absent from their own tradition. Many churches and denominations can find examples in their own histories of the practice of church discipline. Rediscovering radical roots and the stimulus of contemporary groups that are practising church discipline can help us reconsider this subject.

(d) Church planting is a major feature of contemporary church life, even in the West. Establishing new congregations presents a chance to think fresh thoughts about how churches operate. Sadly, in many cases, those involved assume that church planting means "more of the same" rather than planting "new" churches. But there is a "window of opportunity" whenever a new church is planted, as foundations are laid, to build in things that were not practised in the mother church. Establishing a framework for church discipline in a new church is easier than in a church with long-established traditions and expectations. There is less to unlearn. There is often also a pioneering and radical spirit in a new church that will embrace what may be seen as a radical and risky practice.

So there are grounds for hoping that church discipline might be taken seriously and restored as a normal part of church life. In the following chapters, we will explore New Testament teaching on this subject, trying to understand why church discipline is needed, what it can achieve, how it is exercised and what issues it applies to. Our starting point and focus throughout these chapters will be the words of Jesus himself in what deserves to be regarded as the classic exposition of church discipline in the New Testament – Matthew 18.

3

The Process of
Church Discipline

*If your brother sins against you, go and show him his fault,
just between the two of you. If he listens to you, you have
won your brother over. But if he will not listen, take one or
two others along, so that 'every matter may be established
by the testimony of two or three witnesses'. If he refuses to
listen to them, tell it to the church; and if he refuses to listen
even to the church, treat him as you would a pagan or a tax
collector.* (Matthew 18:15-17)

The Gospels record only two occasions when Jesus spoke about
the church. On the first occasion (Matthew 16:17-19) he assured
his disciples that he would build his church and that no external
force would be able to destroy it. On this second occasion he
urged his disciples to take responsibility for this new community
and to ensure that internal problems did not damage the church.

This is the classic passage on church discipline. There are
important teachings elsewhere in the New Testament, to which we
will refer as we explore the subject, but this passage contains all
the main elements of church discipline. Church discipline is not
something that was introduced by the leaders of the early church
as a way of trying to keep control of the expanding movement: it
is rooted in the teaching of Jesus himself and is one of the very
few things we know he wanted to happen in church life.

The context of this passage is important. Matthew has placed it
where he has for a reason. The early part of the chapter (vv. 1-5)
recalls the time when Jesus urged his disciples to be humble like
little children and to welcome children in his name. He went on
(vv. 6-9) to speak strongly about sin, warning them to neither
tolerate sin in their own lives nor cause others to sin. The

following verses (vv. 10-14) record the familiar parable of the lost sheep, where the shepherd searches for the wandering sheep to return it to the fold.

After the passage on church discipline, Matthew repeats Jesus' words about the authority given to the disciples to "bind" and "loose" and adds the words quoted so often when Christians meet together: *"where two or three come together in my name, there I am with them"* (vv. 18-20). The church is where Jesus' presence is experienced and his authority is exercised through his people. The final section (vv. 21-35) contains Peter's question about forgiveness. Jesus' answer that forgiving seventy times seven is nearer the mark than seven times, and the parable of the unmerciful servant, a cautionary tale about receiving and offering forgiveness.

The immediate context of the section on church discipline, then, contains elements that are crucially important when considering this subject: the seriousness of sin, the importance of humility, the Father's concern that none are lost, the authority given to the church to act in Jesus' name and the availability of forgiveness.

The passage itself outlines a process. Church discipline is not a sudden decision or a quick response to a crisis but an expression of pastoral care that may involve a considerable time period and many people. There are distinct stages in this process. We will explore these carefully in order to understand how the process operates and what can be achieved at each stage. Effective church discipline requires that the whole church understands the biblical framework contained in this passage and that the process is worked through carefully, step by step.

Stage 1: Challenge One Another[1]

The first stage of church discipline is best understood as a normal part of church life rather than something exceptional. Church membership means belonging to a community of disciples where

---

[1]The term "admonish" is often used to describe this process, but we have chosen a word that is in more common usage.

there is a responsibility to encourage, instruct, challenge, admonish and rebuke each other. We cannot use Cain's excuse, *"Am I my brother's keeper?"* (Genesis 4:9). We are brothers and sisters in God's family and responsible for each other. Confronting one another, bringing challenge, correction, rebuke and admonition are to be features of our life together. Churches are not social clubs but communities of would-be disciples, who *"spur one another on towards love and good deeds"* (Hebrews 10:24). Many New Testament passages teach this:

> *"Let the word of Christ dwell in you richly as you teach and admonish one another."* (Colossians 3:16)

> *"And we urge you, brothers, warn those who are idle, encourage the timid, help the weak, be patient with everyone."* (1 Thessalonians 5:14)

> *"My brothers, if one of you should wander from the truth and someone should bring him back, remember this: Whoever turns a sinner from the error of his way will save him from death and cover over a multitude of sins."*
> (James 5:19-20)

This is how we should understand the first stage in the process described in Matthew 18. A number of points should be underlined:

(1) Challenging is part of being sisters and brothers together: **if your brothers sins.** Church discipline is not about hostility or antagonism but an expression of brotherly love. You challenge a brother or sister because you care about their spiritual life, because their well-being matters to you, because you want to see them growing as disciples of Jesus – not because you are cross with them. Paul counsels: *"do not regard him as an enemy, but warn him as a brother"* (2 Thessalonians 3:15).

(2) Challenging is the responsibility of all Christians, not just those in leadership positions. A common misunderstanding of the whole process of church discipline is that it is a responsibility that church leaders should shoulder. **But there is no reference to church leaders in this passage.** Church leaders will often be involved in church discipline, as other passages indicate, but to restrict this process to church leaders is to introduce some unhelpful dynamics into what is meant to be a communal process. Church discipline is essentially about relationships between brothers and sisters.

(3) The phrase *if your brother sins against you* has sometimes been seen as an indication that the only person able to bring a challenge is one who has been hurt or offended. Perhaps in many situations this is how the first stage of church discipline will operate. The offence is personal and the offended person goes privately to the person responsible and raises the issue with him or her. But it is unwise to restrict responsibility in this way. The text itself is uncertain, with some manuscripts omitting the words *against you*. More importantly, any sin within the community should concern all the members of the community, both because of its possible impact on the community and because of the potential damage to the sister or brother who has sinned. Furthermore, what should happen if the offended person is not a church member but a neighbour? Surely in this case others would need to intervene to attempt to restore the relationship and ensure that the witness of the church is not damaged. For these reasons, and since no other New Testament passages restrict the process in this way, it is best to recognise that anyone who knows that a brother or sister has sinned has a responsibility towards them.

(4) Challenging requires action: *go and show him his fault.* There will be a natural tendency to hesitate in the hope that such a step will not after all be necessary. Perhaps praying for the person will suffice. Perhaps someone else will take action. While this passage does not suggest that challenging should be hasty or ill-prepared, it does urge action rather than unhelpful dithering. Go and see the brother or sister. Talk through what is concerning you. The word translated *"show him his fault"* might be better translated "reason with him". Although it implies a rebuke, it leaves open the

possibility of discussion and exchange of views. You may be right to be concerned, or you may have misinterpreted the situation, but you will not know until you "go" and find out. What about writing to the person rather than going? Face-to-face action requires courage but is generally better than writing a letter. The goal is a restored relationship. Talking together is more likely to achieve this than an exchange of correspondence, although sometimes a letter setting out your concerns and suggesting a meeting may be a helpful first step. There are examples in Paul's letters of written challenges followed up by personal visits (e.g. 1 Corinthians 4:14-21).

(5) A crucial element at this stage is privacy: *just between the two of you*. Whoever takes the initiative, this is a private matter. There are several reasons for this: it protects the person who has sinned from shame; it prevents damaging gossip that can destroy trust in a community; it allows issues to be explored in confidence so that the facts can be established; the person being challenged may have been misinterpreted. Donald Bridge comments that private action "gives every incentive to make adjustments with the minimum of embarrassment. It tests the motives of the offended party. It gives him no room for gossip or scandal, and puts a bridle on his lips. It offers no leeway to officious busybodies to spread the trouble".[2]

There is a direct correlation in local church life between failure to exercise church discipline and the prevalence of gossip. In any church relationships will become strained at times and people will be offended. If the process of church discipline is not understood and owned by church members, the probable outcome of such tensions will be disunity, back-biting, gossip and broken relationships. Exercising church discipline may be painful at times, but the alternatives are much more painful – and contain none of the healing potential of church discipline. Church discipline protects a community from gossip and restores relationships.

Is it legitimate to ask advice before challenging someone? What if you are wrong? What if you have misinterpreted their actions?

[2]Bridge, Donald: *Spare the Rod and Spoil the Church* (MARC, 1985) p.19.

Some argue that the best way to learn is to go and see but, especially as a church that is unfamiliar with this process learns to exercise church discipline, it may help to be flexible here. There are obvious dangers: avoiding responsibility, indulging in gossip under cover of wanting advice. But if no names or specific details are divulged, it may help to clarify the issues.

(6) The goal of this, as of every stage of the process, is to win the person back, like the shepherd searching for the lost sheep: *if he listens to you, you have won your brother over.* Your purpose is not to win an argument but to win a brother, not to make a complaint but to help a sister make progress as a disciple. If this is achieved, the process immediately comes to a halt and there is joy and celebration as those involved are restored to one another. Further action may be needed to resolve certain issues, to make restitution or to restore other broken relationships, but the brother or sister has been "won". If challenging one another was practised in local churches, many pastoral crises could be averted, many damaging splits could be nipped in the bud, a much higher quality of community life and discipleship could be attained, and the need for the later stages of church discipline would become rarer.

Stage 2: Take a Witness

Private challenges are not always effective. The person who has sinned may not admit to any fault or be willing to change behaviour acknowledged to be wrong. They may even refuse to discuss the matter. Challenging is a risky business with no guarantee of success. But the damage caused by failure to challenge one another is much greater – either sin goes unchecked and relationships are broken, or if this stage is bypassed, issues become public unnecessarily and the process is short-circuited with unhelpful consequences.

But if private action is unsuccessful, the next stage is for one or two others to be involved. The intention is still to keep the matter as confidential as possible in the hope that the brother or sister will be willing to respond positively so that the process of church discipline need progress no further. Again a number of issues should be emphasised:

(1) If you have been unsuccessful in *winning your brother over* through private action you are responsible for taking a further step. There is a temptation to let things rest here rather than pursuing them. Perhaps the situation is less serious than you had thought. Perhaps the person has not sinned after all, or at least not seriously. Perhaps there is nothing to be gained by continuing. Why not let it drop? But unresolved issues of this kind do not disappear. There is a relationship to be restored, there is a sister or brother in need of help, there is an issue to be resolved.

(2) The next step is to *take one or two others along*, drawing them into this confidential matter. Depending on the situation they may or may not be aware of the issue: if they are, they may already be considering approaching the same person. No guidelines are given as to who to draw in – there is no assumption that church leaders should be involved, although this may sometimes be appropriate. The onus is on the one who initiated the process to choose appropriate persons. If concern for the person who has sinned is foremost, rather than self-justification, you will opt for wise and trusted persons rather than those you expect to back you up regardless.

(3) The second stage of the process consists of this small group meeting with the person who has sinned. The purpose is to examine the situation, to confront sinful behaviour and to encourage the sister or brother to resolve this issue. The goal has not changed: you want to win the person, not to cause hurt or damage. There may be several meetings. Neither private challenges nor small group action need be restricted to one attempt. If there is hope of progress, further meetings may be held before the next stage of the process is reached. However, it should be made clear that this cannot go on indefinitely – for the sake of all concerned.

(4) The role of the "witnesses" appears at first glance to be

primarily to support the challenger, to add weight to the case, and to urge the person to respond positively. Their presence implies that this matter will not be allowed to remain unresolved, that a response is needed. It is important that they act carefully so that undue pressure is not exerted. Their role is to express concern for the brother or sister and to urge repentance. They are witnesses rather than judges.

(5) At this point, Jesus quotes from Old Testament law (Deuteronomy 19:15): *every matter may be established by the testimony of two or three witnesses.* This provision was not designed to increase the pressure on those accused of crimes but to protect them. No one could be convicted on the evidence of only one witness. The role of witnesses in church discipline, then, is double-edged. They may support the challenger, but they might exonerate the person being challenged. Perhaps the situation has been misread. Perhaps other factors need to be considered. Perhaps there is fault on both sides. Perhaps there has been repentance but this has not been recognised. The goals of this small group meeting are to help both parties express their perceptions, to work towards the issues being resolved and, if possible, to enable reconciliation to take place.

(6) Although nothing is said about the person being challenged inviting others to act as "witnesses for the defence", this may be appropriate. There may be some who can shed light on the situation, or who can help those already involved better to understand each other. The goal of *"winning your brother"* means that any step consistent with the spirit of Jesus' teaching that might achieve this should be considered.

(7) The familiar promise that *where two or three come together in my name, there am I with them,* should perhaps be rescued from over-use and restored to its biblical context. It assures us that a small group lovingly and patiently meeting together to restore someone who has wandered from the truth, can expect to know the presence of their Lord in a special way. It reminds us also that the authority to "bind" and to "loose" is given to such a

group. There is solemnity about this process, but also great potential for healing and restoration.

A biblical example of this process, although in a situation where there was greater public knowledge than usual, is recorded in Philippians 4:2. Paul asks a church member to help reconcile two sisters whose relationship has evidently broken down. The absence of other examples is probably due to the private nature of such activities. If challenging is taking place as instructed here and is effective, nobody else will know about it.

Stage 3: Tell it to the Church

The refusal of a person to respond positively to a challenge from either an individual or a small group leads on to the next stage in the process of church discipline that Jesus outlines in Matthew 18. From this point the matter becomes public knowledge within the church, and it is now that the maturity of the church, its understanding of the principles of church discipline, and its commitment to the process will be tested.

Several issues need to be explored:

(1) What does it mean to *tell it to the church*? Different views of the church and different systems of church government will affect the way in which this stage is carried through. There are various possibilities: bringing the matter to the notice of the church leaders; putting the issue on the agenda of a church members' meeting; talking personally to every member of the church or house group. At this stage it is important that the church acts together, and so the guidance of the church leaders is essential. However, there is no good reason for restricting this stage to church leaders, as many have done. The matter may be brought to them for presentation to the church, and they may want to discuss this before involving the whole church. But it is important that church leaders do not usurp the role of the community. The focus in Matthew 18 is on **church** discipline, community accountability, rather than on church leaders taking responsibility for exercising discipline. How a church handles church discipline will reveal how seriously it believes in the priesthood of all believers. At every stage the temptation is strong to restrict the process to church leaders.

(**2**) What the church does once it has been told about the situation is to continue the process of challenging the brother or sister. What was previously restricted to one person or a small group now involves the whole church. This could involve a public rebuke and invitation to repentance, or several church members speaking individually to the sister or brother. Since the stated purpose is that he or she should *listen to the church*, clearly the church responds to being informed about the situation by speaking to the person concerned in appropriate ways.

(**3**) This is a tremendously demanding process, for the church as well as for the person concerned. There is plenty of scope for division, gossip, wrong attitudes and confusion. It is not surprising that church leaders sometimes prefer to restrict this stage to themselves. But the impact of the whole church expressing its concern for the person in this way can be tremendous. Nothing should be done that would dilute this.

(**4**) Writing to Timothy about church discipline, Paul instructs his young colleague that church leaders are not exempt from this process of public challenge. The same stipulation regarding two or three witnesses applies to them as to other church members (1 Timothy 5:19). If they do not respond, *"those who sin are to be rebuked publicly, so that the others may take warning"* (1 Timothy 5:20). This stage not only gives the brother or sister another chance to repent, it also acts as a deterrent to others and as a spur to discipleship. Paul himself had practised this form of church discipline. As he tells the Galatians, *"when Peter came to Antioch, I opposed him to his face, because he was clearly in the wrong... I said to Peter in front of them all..."* (Galatians 2:11, 14). Public challenges have a salutary effect upon the whole community as well as being a powerful expression of concern for the person being challenged.

Stage 4: Pagans and Tax Collectors

If he refuses to listen even to the church, treat him as you would a pagan or tax collector. The phrase *"refuses to listen"* is stronger than *"will not listen"* used earlier in the passage. Attitudes have hardened. The response you have been hoping for has not been achieved. The person will not listen "even to the church".

Throughout the process your goals remain the same – "winning" your brother or sister, restoration to fellowship and progress in discipleship. At each stage you hope that this will be the outcome and that no more stages will be needed. But if the person will not listen to the church when the matter is made public, a further stage follows. Instead of being treated as a brother or sister, this person must now be regarded as outside the church, no longer a disciple of Jesus. He or she must be treated as a pagan or a tax collector, groups recognised as outsiders by the Jews in Jesus' day. This stage is sometimes described in terms that sound rather threatening: "excommunication", or "the ban", or "shunning". It is important to understand what this stage in the discipline process means and how it operates:

(a) As with all previous stages in the process, your hope is that there may be a positive response. Putting someone out of the church may seem like rejection, but it should be interpreted rather as respecting their freedom to choose how to live. It acknowledges that they have chosen to live in a way that is inconsistent with being a disciple of Jesus and a member of a community of disciples. Every member is free to make this choice – but not remain as a member of the community as if nothing had changed. Expulsion makes clear the reality of the situation and confronts the person with the implications of their choice. The hope and prayer of the community is that they will come to realise the position they are in and repent. No longer being a member of the community may bring home more powerfully than anything else the danger they are in and the consequences of their choice.

(b) What does treating someone *"as a pagan or a tax collector"* involve? Both groups were despised and avoided by conscientious Jews. Pagans were godless outsiders, tax collectors were collaborators and swindlers. This must mean some kind of distancing, especially if a church takes seriously several other New Testament texts that call for "avoidance" (Romans 16:17; 1 Corinthians 5:11; 2 Thessalonians 3:6; 2 Timothy 3:1-5; Titus 3:9-10). How this is implemented will vary from place to place depending on cultural factors and church structures. Some regard this as requiring exclusion from church meetings; others allow continued attendance at meetings but revoke church membership; others interpret the biblical teaching as banning all social contact with the person. It is important that the church thinks through the implications of the restrictions it imposes and is consistent in practice. It is important also that attitudes towards such persons are carefully guarded. They are not the enemy, but no longer can they be treated as fellow-disciples.

(c) Why does Jesus use the phrase *treat him as you would a pagan or tax collector*? This phrase seems strange on the lips of Jesus, suggesting coolness, even hostility, until we remember who is speaking and how he treated these people. Jesus did distinguish between Jews and pagens but he always reached out to those who reached out to him. He certainly reached out to tax collectors (including Matthew, who perhaps had a smile on his lips as he wrote this section of his Gospel). What Jesus seems to mean here is that the sister or brother who has been excluded should no longer be treated as a church member but as a *potential* church member. He or she is now in need of the gospel like others outside the church. The church's commission to make disciples applies to everyone: those within the church need help to grow as disciples; those outside the church need help to become disciples. The person who has been excluded from the church – however this is expressed – has transferred from one group to the other. He or she is now an outsider who might become an insider.

(d) Whatever exclusion involves in practice, the guiding principles are that the person must know he or she is no longer a member of the church but that the church still loves them. Marlin Jeschke writes: "avoidance must say two things simultaneously, first that a given person has forsaken the way of discipleship; and second, that he or she has a standing invitation to return".[3] This is a difficult balance to attain, but it is important to strive for it. In practice this may mean that the person is excluded from meetings for church members but free to attend public meetings, which are advertised as being open to all. It may allow for continuing friendships with church members, who will hopefully have similar friendships with many who are not church members, provided such contact does not imply that all is well.

(e) One practice that has sometimes been used at this stage, or as an intermediate stage before expulsion, is excluding the person from taking part in communion, but from no other aspect of church life. This is a very unhelpful practice that conveys a mixed message to the person concerned and is a misuse of communion. If practised extensively it would result in two-tier churches of communicants and non-communicants and communion would be regarded as a reward for holy living. Either someone is in fellowship with the community or not. If they are in fellowship, they should not be treated as second-class citizens. If not, full exclusion is needed rather than this partial measure that fudges the issue.

(f) The effectiveness of exclusion from the church will depend on whether the church is worth belonging to. Will exclusion hurt? What will the person miss? How important are the relationships that will no longer be what they were? How meaningful was the worship? Church discipline works best – in fact it only works at all – in a setting where belonging to the church is important enough for exclusion to leave a big hole in a person's life.

(g) We should recognise that in practice exclusion is often little more than a formality, since someone who has refused the admonition of the church is unlikely to be comfortable continuing to participate in its activities. Church membership, after all, is voluntary and members can leave at any time they wish. However, it is important that the church proceeds with the exclusion rather

[3]Jeschke, Marlin: *Discipling in the Church* (Herald 1988) p95.

than feeling that the process of discipline has failed and letting the person leave quietly. This fourth stage is part of the process and should not be omitted. There are several reasons for this.

One reason is so that the person cannot simply slip back in later as if nothing had happened. Alternatively they might approach another church and claim to be in good standing with their previous church. The church should conclude the disciplinary process as an expression of its responsibility towards other churches. Another reason is so that the church is not accused of "sweeping things under the carpet" by allowing a quiet withdrawal. A more important reason is that exclusion has a spiritual as well as a practical significance. Jesus goes on: *"whatever you bind on earth will be bound in heaven."* Other passages speak about this stage as *"passing judgement"* (1 Corinthians 5:3) or as *"handing over to Satan"*[4] (1 Corinthians 5:5; 1 Timothy 1:20). This formal exclusion has a spiritual dimension which is part of the disciplinary process. The church acts in judgement in this situation – and in the hope that through this the person will be brought to repentance.

(h) There are examples in the New Testament of churches excluding members. Paul urges the Thessalonians to expel certain idlers and divisive members (2 Thessalonians 3:6, 14), and tells the Corinthians to expel a man who was involved in sexual immorality (1 Corinthians 5:1-13). In each situation it is clear that the action is not intended to be permanent, but with a view to ultimate restoration. Paul's hope is that the persons involved will be "shamed" into repentance (2 Thessalonians 3:14) and "saved" (1 Corinthians 5:5). Expulsion is an exercise of judgement – but not of final judgement, which belongs to God alone. Winning the brother or sister back remains the purpose of the whole process.

Stage 5: Restoration

Matthew 18 says nothing about restoration. There is no guarantee

[4]Presumably meaning that the person is no longer within the realm of God's authority but back in "the world" of which Satan is currently the prince.

that faithfully working through the process of church discipline will result in restoration, however much the church may long for this. But this does not mean that the process has been ineffective for, as we shall see, church discipline achieves other things as well as attempting to restore those who have sinned.

However, the primary goal is restoration and renewed fellowship with the one who has been disciplined. At each stage of the process, restoration is possible (so "stage 5" may in fact follow stages 1, 2 or 3). Although Jesus says nothing about this in the verses we are studying, we have seen that this passage is set in a context of searching for lost sheep in order to return them to the fold and of forgiving those who ask for mercy. Other passages (e.g. 1 Timothy 1:20) assure us that restoration is both possible and desired. Expulsion from the church is never intended to be permanent.

Churches should be as ready to "loose" as to "bind". Delaying the process of restoration can be as damaging as hesitating to exercise discipline in the first place. Paul's instructions to the Corinthians about expelling a member are as uncompromising as anything in the New Testament on church discipline: *"expel the wicked man from among you"* (1 Corinthians 5:13, quoting, like Jesus, from Deuteronomy 19). But in his second letter to the same church he pleads for the restoration of a man who has been expelled (probably a different man): *"you ought to forgive and comfort him, so that he will not be overwhelmed by excessive sorrow. I urge you, therefore, to reaffirm your love for him"* (2 Corinthians 2:7-8). The church had been slow to challenge someone who was clearly behaving sinfully. Now it was slow to restore someone who was clearly repentant.

Several issues should be understood regarding the process of restoration:

(a) The general principle is that the restoration process should be as public as the church discipline process has been. If the person listens to private challenge or to a small group of witnesses, restoration should take place privately and need not involve the whole church. If the church has been informed, restoration should also be public. Private restoration is relatively straightforward, so the following comments apply mainly to the process of public restoration, although similar principles will apply to the private situation.

(b) Restoration follows a change of heart and a renewed commitment to discipleship by the person who is under discipline. Evidence is needed of repentance, just as evidence of sin was needed for the process of church discipline. How to assess such repentance is not without difficulty. The church cannot see into the person's heart to judge the reality or depth of repentance. Words of repentance must be taken seriously, not treated with suspicion, but changed behaviour and lifestyle are the normal evidence of repentance. Churches will need discernment here and may find it helpful to ask a small group to meet with the person for a period to explore this. This process should neither be rushed nor unduly drawn out, but it is best to regard restoration, like church discipline, as a process rather than something instantaneous. In the context of church discipline, Paul advises Timothy not to be *"hasty in the laying on of hands"* (1 Timothy 5:22).

(c) Certain steps may be needed to express repentance. Restitution may need to be made to those who have been hurt by the person. Some kind of follow-up procedure may be agreed upon to help the person work through the difficulties that resulted in the process of discipline being implemented. Such steps should not be seen as some kind of penance but as an expression of the person's freedom and renewed commitment to discipleship and of the support of the church.

(d) There is also a place for confession by the person being restored, in the same way that new Christians might give testimony to their new-found faith. And like such testimonies, the emphasis should be on the present and the future rather than the past. Although acknowledgement of sin may be appropriate, a healthy confession will concentrate on what God has done and the renewed commitment to discipleship that has resulted. Confession should not be regarded as a punishment but as part of the restoration process – a solemn but joyful affirmation.

(e) The church needs then to respond to this confession by expressing its forgiveness and welcoming the brother or sister back into fellowship. This has spiritual and pastoral dimensions. The church had "bound" the person but now "looses" them. Just as baptism signifies incorporation into the community for new members, so a symbolic act may be appropriate to signify someone's restoration to the community. Possibilities include breaking bread together, with the sister or brother being given a place of honour; the laying on of hands and prayer; the right hand of fellowship (sometimes contrasted with the left boot of fellowship that church discipline is supposed to imply!); or even the neglected rite of footwashing. Churches may want to be more creative. Marlin Jeschke writes of a church that used the parable of the prodigal son as their model: "One man who had left a congregation returned in genuine penitence after five years of estrangement. They literally gave him a new sports coat, had a gold ring made for his finger and celebrated with him over a veal dinner!"[5]

(f) Restoration should be full and final, with the person welcomed back into full church membership. The practice adopted by some churches of not allowing participation in communion or certain other church activities for a period is not helpful. Assessing whether restoration should take place may take time but, once someone is restored, he or she should be fully restored. There must be no second-class citizens in the church. Forgiving and restoring someone who has caused hurt to the community will be a further test of the church's maturity and the extent to which it has truly embraced the principles of church discipline. It may, however, be unwise to appoint this person quickly to a leadership position within the church. This is not because their integrity is in question but for the same reason that new Christians should not be drawn too quickly into leadership: time is needed to build relationships and to concentrate on personal growth in discipleship.

(g) What if someone who has been restored, sins again in the

---

[5]Jeshke, *Discipling* p116.

same way? The church may decide to implement the process of church discipline again. But what if the person is restored again and once more returns to their sinful behaviour? Can the church go on and on in this way? It is no coincidence that Matthew records, straight after the section on church discipline, the question asked by Peter: *"how many times shall I forgive my brother when he sins against me? Up to seven times?"* (Matthew 18:21). The prospect of working through church discipline and restoration even seven times is something many churches would baulk at, but Jesus seems to suggest that there is no limit to this process. The parallel passage in Luke's Gospel is equally insistent: *"If your brother sins, rebuke him, and if he repents, forgive him. If he sins against you seven times in a day, and seven times comes back to you and says, 'I repent', forgive him"* (Luke 17:3-4). The Father forgives his children over and over again, so the church can do no less. Certainly care should be taken to assess the reality of repentance, but restoration must always be a possibility. The church has authority to bind and loose, but not to exclude permanently or to withhold forgiveness.

Matthew 18:15-20 is a remarkable passage. John Howard Yoder has commented that: "It gives more authority to the church than does Rome, trusts more to the Holy Spirit than does Pentecostalism, has more respect for the individual than Humanism, makes more moral standards than Puritanism, is more open to the given situation than the 'New Morality'".[6]

Although there are parallels in other documents (such as the Qumran community's "Manual of Discipline") and some of the principles can be found in Old Testament legislation, the procedure Jesus outlines here has his unique stamp upon it. It is radical, demanding, compassionate and hopeful, a realistic strategy to deal with the broken relationships and failures in discipleship that will from time to time be the sad experience of every church. It challenges nominal Christianity, calls us beyond politeness and defends communities from the destructive effects of gossip and unresolved issues between people. If implemented, it cannot fail to have a profound impact on all aspects of church life.

[6]John Yoder: "Binding and Loosing" in *Concern* 14 (February 1967).

4

The Scope of Church Discipline

So much for the way church discipline (and restoration) operates. But what sins requires this process? None of us is perfect, so should we all be under church discipline most of the time? Or does this process apply only to certain serious sins?

This question has exercised Christians throughout church history and several attempts have been made to categorise sins and show when church discipline is necessary. The traditional approach distinguished "mortal" and "venial" sins. Calvin suggested "intolerable offences" and "tolerable faults". During the medieval period three broad categories of offences requiring church discipline (of the punitive and violent kind) were recognised: schism (disunity), heresy (false teaching) and immorality (wrong behaviour). Generally immorality was tolerated longer than schism or heresy. Church discipline depended first on how the offence was categorised and then on some assessment of how serious it was. Various degrees of seriousness were identified, ranging from "petty" through "serious", "grave", "flagrant" and "notorious" to "heinous". In practice the church tended to tolerate some sins but to outlaw others.

A contemporary attempt to define the scope of church discipline, which produces a similar list, is provided by Daniel Wray. He suggests[1] that church discipline is necessary when:

(1) Christian love is violated by serious private offences;
(2) Christian unity is violated by those who form divisive factions which destroy the peace of the church;

[1]Wray, Daniel: *Biblical Church Discipline* (Banner of Truth 1978) p8-9.

(3)   Christian law is violated by those living scandalous lives;

(4)   Christian truth is violated by those who reject essential doctrines of the faith.

But how does a Christian or a church decide whether an offence is serious or not? What about borderline cases? Which doctrines are essential? How scandalous does behaviour have to become? This approach does not seem to provide adequate guidelines, although it indicates areas where problems frequently occur.

The New Testament does not seem to provide such guidelines either. There is no exhaustive list of offences where church discipline applies, though various examples are given:

(1)   Romans 16:17-18 mentions false teaching and divisive behaviour.

(2)   1 Corinthians 5:11 lists sexual immorality, greed, idolatry, slander, drunkenness and financial dishonesty. 1 Corinthians 6:1-10 adds adultery, male prostitution, homosexual behaviour and theft.

(3)   2 Thessalonians 3:6 warns about idleness and disobedience.

(4)   1 Timothy 1:20 identifies blasphemy. 2 Timothy 2:17-18 reveals the blasphemers to be false teachers who were upsetting the church.

(5)   Titus 3:9-10 deplores quarrelling and divisiveness.

(6)   Revelation 2:2, 14, 20 uncovers false teaching, false apostles and false prophets.

The absence of an exhaustive list or clear guidelines in the New Testament about which sins require church discipline suggests that a different approach is needed. Attempting to distinguish between serious and trivial offences is unlikely to be productive.

Perhaps the best way forward is to recall that church discipline is about making disciples and living together as a community of disciples. Since **any** area of sin is a hindrance to discipleship, and **any** sin might damage relationships with others, **any** area of sin can come within the scope of church discipline. There is no need to try to assess how serious a sin is against some arbitrary scale. What is important is: first, the effect this is having on a person's discipleship; second, the way in which they are dealing with it; and third, the effect it is having on the fellowship,

Marlin Jeschke writes: "On the one hand a person might promptly and sincerely repent of so-called flagrant acts of sin. So the mere act of committing them does not call for excommunication. On the other hand, a person who is impenitent about what might be considered a trivial sin can end in that total loss of spiritual life that calls for exclusion from the community of faith".[2] It may be an act, an attitude or a lifestyle that requires action by a fellow-disciple.

John White and Ken Blue suggest as a guideline that church discipline is necessary "at the point where [sin] becomes evident in a way which hampers mutual fellowship".[3] Church discipline is as much about breaches in relationship as about falling short of certain standards. Concern for a brother or sister and the recognition that your relationship with them is not what it might be will prompt you to action. Your interest is in the person rather than the offence. Your focus is on discipleship and whatever hinders this rather than on sin. This helps keep church discipline within the realm of grace rather than law.

If we accept that any area of sin may potentially be a cause of church discipline, some guidelines are clearly needed to assess whether in a given situation church discipline is necessary:

(1) There must be clear evidence of sin. The testimony of witnesses, acknowledgement by the person concerned, or discernment by the community may all be involved in this. Suspicion and hearsay are not an adequate basis for action. Attempting to judge the secrets of the heart will lead to immense problems. The question is not whether the sin is serious but whether it is evident.

(2) Care must be exercised to distinguish biblical and cultural standards. Throughout its history the church has regarded certain beliefs and practices as wrong in one period only to treat them as

[2]Jeschke, *Discipling* p37.
[3]John White & Ken Blue: *Healing the Wounded* (IVP 1985) p108.

right in another. Several of the more notorious heresies were arguably cultural expressions of orthodox Christianity rather than false doctrine. Christians from different cultures today disagree over whether certain practices are acceptable or not (for example, drinking alcohol, smoking, styles of clothing). Multicultural churches must be particularly careful if the norms of the majority culture are not to be imposed on minorities: this is oppression, not church discipline. Enforcing conformity, nit-picking and concentrating on externals can all lead churches into legalism rather than liberty.

(3) The only sins that require church discipline are sins that have not been repented of. The goal of church discipline is not to punish those who have already acknowledged their faults, but to help those who are still captive to sins they are not yet willing to confront. If repentance has already begun, no matter how "serious" the sin, church discipline is inappropriate. The crucial issue is not how someone has behaved but in which direction he or she is now facing – towards Christ or away from him.

This has sometimes been poorly understood by churches that have tried to exercise church discipline. Paul Hiebert, a Christian anthropologist, has identified four ways in which communities define their boundaries: the **open set**, where there are no boundaries; the **fuzzy set**, where boundaries are unclear or inconsistent; the **bounded set**, where boundaries are precise and static, and the **centred set**, where boundaries are directional rather than locational – it matters less where you are than where you are going[4].

Applied to church discipline, the first two sets describe churches where church discipline is rarely or never exercised, either because the distinction between church and society is absent or because there is no framework for church discipline. The third set describes churches which practise church discipline and where acceptable and unacceptable doctrine and behaviour are clearly spelled out, but within a rigid framework that tends

[4]Hiebert's categories are used as a basis for discussing church discipline in Shenk, David & Statzman, Ervin: *Creating Communities of the Kingdom* (Herald Press 1988) pp103-104.

towards legalism and cultural absolutes.

The centred set describes the approach presented here. The community does have boundaries and a framework for church discipline, but the question is not whether someone has acted in a certain way at some point but what their attitude is now. Do they still want to be a disciple? How are they dealing with the area of sin? If there is evidence of repentance, church discipline is inappropriate, though pastoral support and prayer may be.

(4) Any issue, then, that might hinder discipleship or cause a breach in relationships may require some form of church discipline. There are no private areas beyond the reach of church discipline: issues in the family and the workplace as well as in church life fall within its scope. The New Testament seems to envisage three situations where an individual is responsible for initiating this. First, when you believe you have been sinned against (Luke 17:4); second, when you believe that a brother or sister is not living as a disciple, even if this has not directly affected you (Matthew 18:15); and third, when you believe that someone else has something against you (Matthew 5:23-24). This is fairly comprehensive. Whether you believe you have been sinned against or might have given offence to someone else, you are responsible for taking action. Even where you are not directly affected, you accept the responsibility of being your "brother's (or sister's) keeper" and take action.

In each case the word "believe" has been used, not to imply that we should act on suspicion or hearsay, but to acknowledge that how we perceive a situation may be inaccurate. If we are concerned about one another, we will neither jump to conclusions nor fail to take action. The way to check out our concern is to go to the person in question and discuss the issue. Where a community is practising church discipline effectively, it is not impossible that the person will already be on their way to see you.

5

The Purpose of
Church Discipline

The primary purpose of church discipline is restoration. Restoration has two aspects: restoring someone to a life of discipleship and restoring broken relationships within the Christian community. Previous chapters have explored this and insisted that biblical church discipline is not vindictive but an expression of brotherly love; not a way to rid the community of a troublesome member but to restore a friend and fellow-disciple. At each stage of the process there is an opportunity to be restored. Even when all the stages have been worked through, the door remains open.

In this chapter we will briefly examine other purposes that church discipline achieves. These are important and clearly taught in the New Testament, but they must not usurp restoration as the main purpose of church discipline. If other reasons for exercising church discipline assume first place, as they sometimes have, the whole process can become distorted or even vicious. There are enough cases in church history of horrendous applications of church discipline to act as warnings in this area. Restoration is the primary purpose of church discipline.

But church discipline does not always result in restoration. Some people leave the church and do not return. Their hearts of course are known only to God, but from the perspective of the church a sister or brother has been lost. This does not mean, however, that the process has failed. Church discipline serves a number of other functions:

(1) Purifying the church. One of the most intimate descriptions of the church in the New Testament is the Bride of Christ. The destiny of the church is to share eternity with her heavenly

Bridegroom, and her calling in this engagement period is to be faithful and to grow in love for, and friendship with Christ. This image of the Bride is sometimes used to remind the church of the need for purity (2 Corinthians 11:2; Revelation 19:7-8). The church is to be holy, committed to purity, truth, integrity and consistency. This is how she prepares for her wedding day.

Church discipline is a means of removing impurities. In his letter to the church at Corinth, Paul spells this out. After expressing outrage that the church was tolerating immoral behaviour that *"does not occur even among pagans"* (1 Corinthians 5:1), he continues:

> *Don't you know that a little yeast works through the whole batch of dough? Get rid of the old yeast that you may be a new batch without yeast – as you really are. For Christ, our Passover lamb, has been sacrificed. Therefore let us keep the Festival, not with the old yeast, the yeast of malice and wickedness, but with bread without yeast, the bread of sincerity and truth… "Expel the wicked man from among you".*   (1 Corinthians 5:6-8, 13)

Removing sin from the church is important if it is to be pure. It will not do to dismiss this as an idealistic attempt to produce a perfect church, an accusation that has often been levelled against those who have dared to practise church discipline. Concern for a pure church should not be confused with a holier-than-thou attitude or perfectionism. Indeed, to practice church discipline is to recognise that the church is **not** perfect. But while a perfect church may be unattainable in this age, a process that recognises human frailty but holds on to the vision of the church as the pure and faithful Bride of Christ is vital. The alternative is compromise and disillusionment.

(2) Maintaining the testimony of the church. The purity of the church is important not only because of its ultimate calling and destiny, but also to enable it to fulfil its commission to make disciples. Tolerating sin leads to confusion, weakness and division in the church. People do not know where they stand. The church's ability to help its members live as disciples is reduced. Furthermore, the church's witness in the community is damaged. Many people outside the church have high expectations of Christians, and the accusation of hyprocrisy because churches do not practice what they preach is frequent and in many cases justified. John Stott has written: "The secular world is almost wholly unimpressed by the Church today... So long as the Church tolerates sin in itself and does not judge itself... it will never attract the world to Christ."[1]

The fear that a church which exercises church discipline will not prove attractive in a climate of tolerant liberalism may be unfounded. Some will doubtless be dissuaded from joining, but others will be drawn to a church where love is expressed in the form of mutual accountability. This double response is clear in the New Testament. After the incident which saw the removal of Ananias and Sapphira from the church, we read (Acts 5:13-14) that *"no-one else dared join them, even though they were highly regarded by the people. Nevertheless, more and more men and women believed in the Lord and were added to their number"*.

(3) Deterring others. The practice of church discipline has a salutary effect on the church. A community where consistent standards are upheld, where compromise is not tolerated, where sin is not treated as a private matter, provides a challenging but secure environment for those who want to be disciples. Challenging, because of the responsibility both to give and receive admonition. Secure, because there are brothers and sisters who will not leave you to struggle alone with failure and lethargy.

The New Testament mentions this by-product of church discipline (and by-product it is, for church discipline is never to be seen as "making an example of someone"). Paul tells Timothy that public rebukes are necessary on occasions, *"so that the others may take warning"* (1 Timothy 5:20). And the reason Paul confronted Peter publicly in Antioch was not only to challenge his behaviour, which he could have done in private, but to warn those who were being led astray by Peter's behaviour (Galatians 2:11-13).

---

[1]Stott, John: *Confess Your Sins* (Word 1974) p49.

(4) Deflecting God's judgement. The choice seems clear: either the church exercises judgement or God will. If a church refuses to exercise discipline it may find God himself taking action. Paul warns the Corinthians: *"if we judged ourselves, we would not come under judgement"* (1 Corinthians 11:31). Their failure to judge themselves and put right their relationships had resulted in sickness and even death in the community (v30). A similar warning is spelled out even more clearly by Jesus himself in his messages to the seven churches in Revelation. The importance of church discipline to Jesus surely cannot be in doubt: not only is a significant proportion of his recorded teaching about the church in the Gospels taken up with this subject, but the only direct words of Jesus to individual churches contained in the New Testament emphasise the importance of church discipline.

The church at Ephesus is commended for exposing some false apostles and for rejecting false teachings (Revelation 2:2, 6). But the churches in Pergamum and Thyatira are criticised for failing to exercise church discipline over issues that required this: false teachings and compromised behaviour (Revelation 2:14-15, 20). The church at Pergamum is given a final chance to act but is warned that if it does not, *"I will soon come to you and fight against them with the sword of my mouth"* (Revelation 2:16). For the church at Thyatira there is no further opportunity. Now Jesus himself will take action to bring church members to repentance, so that *"all the churches will know that I am he who searches hearts and minds, and I will repay each of you according to your deeds"* (Revelation 2:23).

These are solemn words. However much or little we may be concerned that the church is pure, Jesus is committed to having a holy bride fit to share his kingdom. Judgement will happen one way or another, but God's intention is that the church should judge itself and exercise discipline so that he does not have to intervene in the ways described in these passages.

Purifying the church, maintaining its distinctive testimony, deterring others and deflecting God's judgement all sound rather threatening and certainly underline the biblical teaching that church discipline is both serious and vitally important. Occasionally in the New Testament, church discipline is referred to as "passing judgement" (e.g. 1 Corinthians 5:3) or as a punishment (e.g. 2 Corinthians 2:6-7), although it is clear in these passages that the intention is always remedial. But these aspects are given relatively little attention in the New Testament compared to the main agenda which is to help one another continue as disciples of Jesus.

Other writers draw attention to two further aspects of church discipline. Marlin Jeschke insists that church discipline in really a special kind of evangelism, confronting people with the claims of Christ and the good news of freedom from sin.[2] Evangelism happens as the church obeys Christ's call to *"go and make disciples"*; church discipline takes place as the church obeys Christ's call to *"go to your brother"*. There are many parallels. The parables of the lost sheep, the lost coin and the lost son (Luke 15) can all be interpreted as illustrations of evangelism or as illustrations of church discipline and restoration. The goal of both is to liberate people from sin and enable them to live as disciples of Jesus in fellowship with God and the church.

John White and Ken Blue include freedom as one of the four goals of church discipline (alongside restoration, reconciliation and purification). Sin binds people and oppresses them. Church discipline is a means by which we can be helped into freedom and full liberty as children of God. Although there are no New Testament passages that explicitly refer to freedom as a goal or result of church discipline, this is clearly another aspect of the restoration that church discipline aims to achieve.

Donald Bridge helpfully sums up the purpose of church discipline: "It is the serious attempt to preserve the truth, order and standards of New Testament Christianity in the local church. It is the determination to take the Son of God seriously, and to harken to his apostles. It is designed for the preservation of spiritual life, the authentication of the church's witness, the discouragement of sin, and the restoration of the fallen".[3]

[2]Jeschke, *Discipling* p16 and throughout his book.

[3]Bridge, *Spare* p159.

6

Practising
Church Discipline

It will not do to describe the process of church discipline as if this is simply a set of rules to be applied. Church discipline is an expression of love and commitment. It is rooted in concern for a fellow-disciple and the way in which the process operates is as important as the process itself. The New Testament gives guidelines on our **attitudes** towards discipline, as well as instructions on what should be done and by whom.

Church discipline exercised in a bad spirit or with wrong motives will not only be ineffective but extremely damaging. Churches that choose to take church discipline seriously are committing themselves to a process which has tremendous potential to do good or to create havoc. As we have seen, fear of making mistakes and knowledge of situations where mistakes have been made, discourage churches from getting involved in church discipline at all. But, as always, the remedy for abuse is not disuse but proper use. Exercising church discipline badly and not exercising it at all both have dire consequences. Learning to manage the process effectively is the way forward.

Crucial attitudes in relation to church discipline include the following:

(1) Church discipline should be exercised **gently** and **humbly**. There is no room for arrogance, self-righteousness or judgemental attitudes (the characteristics of the main alternative to exercising church discipline – gossip). Paul writes: *"Brothers, if someone is caught in a sin, you who are spiritual should restore him gently. But watch yourself, or you also may be tempted. Carry each other's burdens and in this way you will fulfil the law of Christ"* (Galatians 6:1-2). Those involved in the process of church discipline, whether at the stage of private admonition or in the later more public stages, are to act with graciousness and sensitivity.

To become overbearing or angry, to threaten or accuse, to look down on someone or to be insensitive to their feelings, is to fail your brother or sister in their time of need. Instead of sharing the burden, you will add to it. They are already struggling with the demands of discipleship; they do not need you to act like the Pharisees criticised by Jesus because they *"tie up heavy loads and put them on men's shoulders but they themselves are not willing to lift a finger to move them"* (Matthew 23:4). Church discipline involves confrontation and straight talking but this must be done with gentleness and humility. The aim is to heal and restore, not to wound or drive away.

The humility comes from realising that you too may fall into temptation. You may be admonishing your sister today, but you may need her help tomorrow. Church discipline is not a one-way process. Paul encourages those who are "spiritual" to exercise church discipline. This is not an escape clause for those who feel unspiritual, nor should admonition be left to church leaders. Church discipline is a responsibility of the whole church. Being "spiritual" in this situation requires us to examine our own lives, removing any beams in our own eyes so that we can see clearly to remove the specks in our brother's eye (Luke 6:41-42). Being "spiritual" means that we go to our brother or sister prayerfully and in dependence on the Holy Spirit to give us the right words to speak.

(2) Church discipline should be exercised with **grief** and **sorrow**. Your friend is in trouble and in danger. Sin is already damaging one life and now threatens the church. There is no room for complacency, Paul tells the Corinthians. *"Shouldn't you rather have been filled with grief?"* (1 Corinthians 5:2). Church discipline is never easy, especially if the early stages produce no response. Public admonition and the expulsion of someone from the church are very painful. For those involved and for the church as a whole there will be sorrow, deep concern, a sense of loss and a process of grieving. The church may be called to prayer and fasting. Tears will be shed.

Admonition may include pleading as well as rebuke. Paul's second letter to Corinth is a form of church discipline, a letter of admonition. A verse often used in an evangelistic context is actually a plea for a response to admonition: *"We are therefore Christ's ambassadors, as though God were making his appeal through us. We implore you on Christ's behalf: Be reconciled to God"* (2 Corinthians 5:20). This is the spirit of church discipline, pleading for a response, deeply concerned for the person in need, expressing the heart of God.

(3) Church discipline should not treat people as **enemies**. Because it involves confrontation, there is a real danger of hostility. The person being admonished may respond in this way, or the admonisher may become hostile if there is no positive response. Paul reminded the Thessalonians to be wary of this as they exercised church disciplines: *"do not regard him as an enemy, but warn him as a brother"* (2 Thessalonians 3:15).

This is important at every stage. While someone remains within the church they are to be regarded as a brother or sister. If expelled from the church they should be treated as a potential brother or sister, someone God still loves and the church continues to pray for. Even when the situation becomes tense, when the church is slandered for its stance on an issue, when the response to the process is apparently wholly negative, the person involved must not be regarded as the enemy – or else the real enemy will have a field day. A forgiving attitude is essential in the exercise of church discipline.

(4) Church discipline should be exercised with **clarity** and **firmness**. All involved should know what is happening and why. Mixed messages, confusion and indecision at any stage are damaging to all concerned. The issues need to be identified clearly, and the process of church discipline needs to be followed through steadily. This is the main responsibility of church leaders in the process – not to act on behalf of the congregation but to ensure that the process is carefully carried through by the congregation. The need to be gentle and gracious does not preclude this clarity. Church discipline involves *"speaking the* *truth in love"* (Ephesians 4:15).

This is Paul's message to the Corinthians: stop dithering, call a church meeting, put the man out of the church (free translation of 1 Corinthians 5:2-5). The process set out by Jesus is clear and gives every opportunity for a positive response before public action is taken. But if there is none, firm action is required. The church needs to keep its nerve and act decisively. It is also important that explanations are given. The issues must be addressed, not swept under the carpet. Confidentiality is crucial in the early stages, full disclosure is vital in the later stages. This does not mean rehearsing every detail, but it does mean talking honestly abut the issues involved.

(5) Church discipline should allow for **flexibility**. The process described in Matthew 18 is best treated as a framework rather than a straight-jacket. Each occasion for church discipline is unique, and love for the person concerned will require creative and sensitive application of this framework. For example, the amount of time spent on each stage may vary considerably. It may quickly become clear that admonition is achieving nothing and the whole process may take place in a short period. In other situations the early stages may involve several meetings over a period of weeks or months.

In some circumstances some of the stages may become irrelevant. If the disciplinary issue becomes public knowledge, "telling it to the church" may either be unnecessary or be brought forward. If the person involved leaves the church, the admonition stages may be impossible. There seems to be such flexibility in the New Testament. There is no indication Paul had spoken privately or with witnesses to Peter before publicly confronting him about his attitude to the Gentiles (Galatians 2:11).

We must be careful. Flexibility is important, but so is the framework. Normally the steps outlined by Jesus should be taken one by one. The principles are clear and consistent throughout the New Testament, even if their practical application requires wisdom and sensitivity to each situation.

(6) Church discipline should operate within an atmosphere of

acceptance and **forgiveness**. Only a community committed to unconditional love for sinful people and to persistent forgiveness of one another will find church discipline working effectively. Sadly many churches are plagued by legalism, judgemental attitudes, resentments, gossip and division. They are not the reconciled and reconciling communities they might be. Newcomers do not find them accepting communities. In this context, church discipline can be oppressive and destructive.

In such a church introducing admonition may not be the place to start! Paul encourages the church at Colossus to practise admonition, but only in the context of committed relationships:

> *"Therefore, as God's chosen people, holy and dearly loved, clothe yourselves with compassion, kindness, humility, gentleness and patience. Bear with each other and forgive whatever grievances you may have against one another. Forgive as the Lord forgave you. And over all these virtues put on love, which binds them all together in perfect unity. Let the peace of Christ rule in your hearts, since as members of one body you were called to peace. And be thankful. Let the word of Christ dwell in you richly as you teach and admonish one another…"* (Colossians 3:12-16)

This passage describes many of the attitudes we have suggested as vital for effective church discipline. It points us to Jesus as the model for relationships within the Christian community. Only in this kind of church can the potential of church discipline be realised.

This seems very demanding. No wonder so few churches exercise discipline. No wonder some that do have made mistakes and caused damage. We may find ourselves asking with Paul, *"who is equal to such a task?"* (2 Corinthians 2:16). But the New Testament clearly expects churches to tackle this issue – even churches like the one at Corinth where there were so many problems. Church discipline is not for perfect churches (which would then not need to exercise it!). But it does require much from churches.

How might a church begin? What steps are needed to introduce the process of church discipline, or to revive such a process if it has been used unwisely or has fallen into disuse? This is something that will require action from church leaders, so the following suggestions are directed towards those in leadership positions. If you are not, you may need to ask your church leaders to consider this issue.

(a) Lay a clear foundation of teaching on the subject. It is crucial that the church understands why and when church discipline is needed, how it operates, the attitudes necessary for it to be effective, its aims and purposes, and what can go wrong. Without a framework to guide the church, attempts to exercise church discipline can lead to all kinds of problems. Leaders who suddenly discover church discipline and attempt to introduce it without laying a proper foundation are heading for trouble. Teach it, discuss it, consider the legal implications, set out a clear statement that represents the agreed policy of the church. This is an issue on which there must be substantial agreement, if not consensus, if it is to work properly. Enthusiastic leadership is not enough. After all, you are asking church members to take on board something that was not in view when they joined the church. You may even need to disband the membership and invite people to join up again on the new basis of belonging to a community that practises church discipline.

(b) Taking Colossians 3:12-16 as a guide, work towards the church becoming the kind of forgiving and loving community described there. Encourage the development of these attitudes. Challenge church members to deal with any areas of resentment or unforgiveness. However, do not expect a perfect church before you exercise church discipline. Exercising church discipline will go hand in hand with growth in other areas.

(c) Encourage a culture where the truth is spoken in love. Confronting people over sin may not be the place to start. What about asking people to say what they appreciate about each other? It has been suggested that a ratio of 10:1 is appropriate for encouragement and admonition. Or you could encourage people to evaluate your ministry, your preaching, your pastoral care. This might be painful (and revealing), but it may help people break through the barriers of politeness and reticence and learn how to admonish in a constructive way.

(**d**) Keep in view the goal of making disciples. Church discipline is not the only means for achieving this, but it is a means. Develop in the minds of church members a consciousness that the church is a community of disciples, where all are responsible for each other. Incorporating a pledge to this effect in baptismal services (as the Anabaptists did in the sixteenth century) or when welcoming new members into the church might be a helpful foundation and frequent reminder.

(**e**) Act responsibly when receiving those wanting to transfer membership from another church. Are they in good standing with the church they have come from? Why did they leave? Are there unresolved issues that should be tackled before they join a new church? Communicate with a leader in the other church and ask the same questions. If local churches regularly acted in this way, church discipline could be exercised more effectively.

(**f**) If these foundations are well laid, church discipline – at least in its admonition stages – should begin to happen. When a situation arises where the full process needs to be implemented, the church will have a framework of understanding, will have begun to learn how to speak the truth in love and will hopefully be able to pull together and see the process through. The first occasion will be a learning process and an opportunity to reflect together on the lessons learned will be helpful. The risks involved will remain – but they are nowhere near as great as the risks involved in failing to exercise discipline or trying to exercise discipline with an unprepared church.

(**g**) Finally, be prepared for some radical changes. Seriously grappling with the subject of church discipline will challenge many areas of church life. How large can a church grow and still practise church discipline? What role do the leaders have and what responsibilities belong to the whole congregation? What else will a Christian community begin to find in the New Testament as it discovers the implications of "speaking the truth in love" and taking responsibility for one another? Introducing church discipline may be just the beginning…

For Further Reading

Bonhoeffer, Dietrich: *The Cost of Discipleship* (SCM, 1959)
Bridge, Donald: *Spare the Rod and Spoil the Church* (MARC, 1985)
Coffey, David: *Build That Bridge* (Kingsway, 1986)
Jeschke, Marlin: *Discipling in the Church* (Herald Press, 1988)
Lindsell, Stuart: *Relationships – Jesus Style* (Word, 1992)
White, John & Blue, Ken: *Healing the Wounded* (IVP, 1985)
Wray, Daniel: *Biblical Church Discipline* (Banner of Truth, 1978)

Appendix:
Applying the Principles

No examples of situations involving church discipline have been given in preceding chapters. Some of those who kindly read through those chapters have asked why. Wouldn't some examples help to illustrate how the various principles we have identified actually work out in practice?

Yes, they would. The difficulty I face is that to give examples, even with changed names and circumstances, would breach confidentiality. Since I have only been in leadership in one church where church discipline was exercised, it would be all too easy to identify people or situations I might use as examples. Since I have argued that confidentiality is vital in the process of church discipline, in order to provide protection and security for all involved, I can hardly provide examples that breach my own guidelines!

I offer as an alternative some case studies. These are not consciously based on any real-life situations in which I have been involved. They are intended as illustrations of the kinds of issues faced by churches at different stages of the process of church discipline. Hopefully they will pick up significant points from earlier chapters and provide a helpful basis for discussion. These case studies do not lend themselves to easy answers. Church discipline is often complex and requires prayerful discernment rather than a legalistic application of principles. The principles set the parameters but leave considerable room for manoeuvre – a liberating but frightening space for pastoral creativity.

With each of these case studies, then, I suggest that first the basic principles are identified and then the various practical implications are explored. What are you aiming to achieve? And how are you going to move towards those goals? You can study these scenarios yourself or they may be useful starters for group discussions.

In a church where the principles of church discipline are not familiar, it might be helpful to use these case studies as an introduction to this issue. They could be provided for small group study before teaching is given on the subject of church discipline, then used again following the teaching programme. Comparing the groups' responses to the issues raised in the case studies before and after the teaching may help you discover how clearly you have communicated and to what extent this teaching has been embraced.

Case Study 1: Starting Again

Two years ago Central Baptist Church was rocked by the discovery that for almost a decade their treasurer had been falsifying the accounts and diverting church funds into his own account. The facts came to light when the treasurer's teenage daughter told one of the deacons in confidence what she thought was happening. The deacon reported the matter to a specially convened deacons' meeting, to which the treasurer was not invited. The minister visited the treasurer, who initially protested his innocence but then admitted what he had done. He expressed sorrow and a desire to put things right. The minister prayed with him and suggested they meet again a week later to talk further.

The following Sunday the treasurer was quickly aware that many people were avoiding him or giving him strange looks. It was clear that what he had done was now widely known. That was the last church meeting the treasurer attended. Within six months he had moved with his family to another part of the country. His daughter said that she never wanted to set foot inside a church again. The minister tried on several occasions to talk with the treasurer but he refused to see him.

At several deacons' meetings the issue was discussed and regrets were expressed that they had not handled the situation well. They decided not to press charges or ask for repayment of the stolen money, nor did they feel they could do anything more once the treasurer had moved away. The issue of confidentiality was not discussed at any length: it was regarded as sad but inevitable that "these things get out".

Two years on, following study on the subject, the minister has proposed that the church adopts a church discipline policy to enable it to deal more wisely with any similar issue in the future. He has suggested the deacons might review the case of the treasurer and learn from it.

What mistakes were made? Where did things start to go wrong? How could the situation have been rescued? If it happened again, what would they do differently?

Case Study 2: If She Will Not Listen

If had been a difficult two weeks. First there had been the soul searching about whether to confront Joan or let the matter go. After all, she had sometimes said cutting things to other people herself, but Joan seemed to be upsetting so many people and especially those who were new to the church. She decided she had to say something. She had plucked up courage to talk to Joan but was still reeling from the shock of her response. She had never expected to hear such language and she had almost been thrown out of the house. She had stopped crying now but the words were still ringing in her ears – "trouble-maker", "hypocrite", "holier-than-thou", "busybody".

What should she do now? She wished she had left the whole thing alone, but nobody else seemed to be doing anything and she couldn't let Joan go on upsetting young Christians. It was so confusing. She had done what she felt was right but it looked like she had made matters worse.

She needed to talk to someone, to ask advice about what to do next. Who should she go to? One of the elders? Her home group leader? Or should she discuss things with her prayer partner – who was a good friend of Joan's? Or should she just let the whole thing drop and hope someone else would talk to Joan?

What should she do? What would you do? Do you agree with what she has already done?

Case Study 3: A Question of Culture?

Steve and Sally had come to faith in Christ two years ago through the patient witness of a Christian who worked with Steve. Together with their four young children, they had joined the parish church. They were made to feel very welcome and enjoyed the services, but they struggled to bridge the culture gap. After all, they couldn't read very well and it wasn't easy to follow the service book or even the words of the songs as they came up on the screen. But they were making good friends and felt they were growing in faith and understanding.

They liked Bill, the curate, and his wife Sandra and they were pleased to see them when they called in one evening. But they soon discovered that this was not just a social visit. Bill started by saying how encouraged he was with the progress they had been making as Christians since they had joined the church. But he was concerned about certain things and felt he should talk with them about these issues. In particular, he knew they both smoked quite heavily and that Sally went to Bingo twice a week. Was this a sensible use of their money? How did they feel about gambling? Of much greater concern to him was the fact that they were not legally married. He knew they had been living together for years and had assumed they were a married couple, but Sandra had heard from a friend of Sally's recently that this was not so.

Steve and Sally were unsure how to react. They could tell Bill was not trying to make trouble and that he was concerned for their welfare. But what was wrong with smoking and Bingo? They needed to relax sometimes. As for their not being married, what difference did a piece of paper make? They hadn't had much money at the time and decided not to bother with the expense of a proper wedding. Who had told Sandra anyway and why?

Are Bill and Sandra acting wisely here? Are any of these issues matters for church discipline, or just cultural differences? How should Steve and Sally respond? What should Bill and Sandra do next?

Case Study 4: Telling the Church

Agape Christian Fellowship had grown over the past twelve years from a small group meeting in a home to a church of some 275 people meeting in three congregations across the town. The leadership team, which covered all three congregations, was led by Margaret and was due to meet this evening. Margaret was in her study preparing for the meeting.

The main item on the agenda was a painful church discipline issue. Three months earlier she had wept with Judy as she heard how Judy's husband, Peter, had left her and had moved in with Fiona, a single woman in the church. Several visits to Peter and Fiona, on her own and accompanied by two other leaders, seemed to have achieved little except to harden their determination to carry on with this relationship. They had also told her that if the leaders made a public statement criticising them they would go straight to the local press and accuse the church of being judgemental.

Margaret was clear in her own mind that the next step was to explain the situation to the church. But how should this be done? Should all three congregations be informed or just the one to which Peter, Judy and Fiona belonged? What should the church be asked to do, if anything? How would Judy feel about the situation? How seriously should they take the threat made by Peter and Fiona? How would this affect the church's reputation in the area?

What would you advise Margaret to propose to her leadership team?

Case Study 5: Welcome Back

Richard had just put the telephone down when it rang again. This time it was one of the deacons, Tony, who had also received a telephone call from a seemingly repentant David. A year earlier David had been disciplined by the church for being persistently divisive, spreading rumours about several members and refusing to respond to all attempts to help him confront this issue. David had stayed away from church activities and had had little contact with members of the church. Now he had rung both Richard and Tony to say that God had spoken to him about his behaviour and that he wanted to apologise to the church and be restored to membership.

Richard and Tony compared notes and discovered that while David had said almost exactly the same to each of them about his change of heart, he had given Richard the impression that he expected Richard to be cautious about restoring him but had told Tony that he felt sure Tony would want to act on this straight away. How should they interpret this? Was David still trying to be divisive? Was this deliberate or just bad habit? Or were they reading too much into his words?

Richard and Tony continued to discuss the situation. How could they test his new attitude? How soon should they allow him to talk to the church? Should they let him say what he wanted or talk it through with him first? If his change of heart was genuine, how should they mark his restoration to membership? This was the first time anyone they had disciplined had asked to return – an exciting development if he was sincere. How could they use this as a learning experience for the church and as a time of healing and restoration for David? What should they encourage church members to do, especially those who had been hurt by David?

How would you advise Richard and Tony?

❖ ❖ ❖ ❖